AF454159

# Ease Your Life

## The Wellness Guided Journal

Najja Ogunshola

# Contents


Introduction                                    IV

Part One: Health                                 1

Part Two: Emotional Freedom                     20

Part Three: Mental Freedom                      42

The Last Step: Your Five-Year Plan              67

# Introduction

Have you been feeling as though you are in a rut? Perhaps you have been feeling like the routine is getting old, and as though there is no *novelty* in your life. Each day feels the same. You are constantly watching YouTube videos of people who inspire you and you find yourself wishing that you were like them, with their extensive morning and night routines, their ability to wake up early and do more before 9 a.m. than you do in your whole day and their infinite energy. You might also see how well they take care of themselves, and you may think to yourself, *wow, I'm not doing enough for myself.*

But then again, you feel overwhelmed. *How am I supposed to get up at 5 a.m., go to the gym, drink my green juice but not too much juice because it's bad for weight loss, and then go home and make myself a healthy breakfast but not too healthy because that's diet culture, and walk ten thousand steps a day but also don't just do it inside because you need the sun, and then do my ten-step skincare routine, and also make sure to do mindfulness and gratitude exercises throughout the day, and, and, and...*

It's overwhelming, the amount of information we have coming our way when it comes to health and wellness. It's hard to think about *all the things we need to do*, when in reality, most of us aren't influencers with a schedule that we can choose to organize our own way.

And yet, health and wellness are simple. It's about taking care of our body in a holistic way. It's about making choices that align with how we want to *feel*. It's about eating in a way that makes us feel good and moving in a way that helps our body thrive. It's not about doing the 75Hard challenge and burning out, only to go back to the bad habits we had before, or about doing crash diets that make us feel good about the short-term weight loss but feel bad about binging later on because we have deprived our body of the nutrients it *craves* to function well.

If you can relate to all of this, this workbook is perfect for you. It was created to help you develop a stronger and healthier relationship with your body. In fact, I structured it in three specific parts to help you revisit how you view your health and wellness, and to help you step away from the ideas that have been ingrained in us after years of growing up in diet culture. From the day you start this workbook to the end of your journey with it, you will start shifting the way you view your life and your relationship to wellness.

To do this, we will be looking at health and wellness in terms of three overarching concepts: **health, emotional freedom, and mental freedom. Health** is specifically related to your body-mind connection, self-care, and healing through movement. It invites you to view your body as the vessel that carries you through life, as opposed to a separate being that you want to change *so badly*. It likewise welcomes you to the idea of healing through movement so you can begin to feel more connected to yourself.

Then, **emotional freedom** focuses on how your emotions are connected to your body. For example, it focuses on the emotional baggage that you may be carrying, and whether it is affecting the current state of your body. It looks at how to embrace vulnerability as a way to be more mindful and connected to yourself. It invites you to be compassionate, instead of critical, of yourself.

Finally, **mental freedom** is something many of us struggle to reach. We are shackled by the rules of society around how we need to take care of ourselves, or how we need to appear to *others*. Imagine a world in which you are free from your limiting beliefs, where you are mindful of how you feel and how external aspects affect this. Importantly, imagine how the world may feel if you detached yourself from external validation!

This workbook is a combination of activities and prompts to help you rethink how you view yourself and the world, and how these views impact your overall wellbeing and health. Being *healthy* is so much more than being in a body you like—it's about ensuring that you nurture your mind, emotions, and overall health *holistically*, namely by recognizing that these are all interconnected.

Are you ready to make some changes?

# Part One: Health

Welcome to the first part of this workbook. This first part is all about your health, specifically about how to become more in touch with yourself, your body, and how you treat it. If you have long been part of diet culture or have thought about how you *look* as opposed to how you *feel* many times in your life, chances are that you will need some time to adjust to this new way of thinking. Instead of thinking about how you want to *look* in the future, think about how you want to *feel* in the future, once you have taken up new habits that make you feel good about yourself and make you feel like you can do anything, unrestricted by the limits inflicted by your body. We'll start with the body-mind connection and will then move on to self-care as an act of self-respect. Finally, we will look into how you can use movement to heal.

## The Body-Mind Connection

The prompts in this section are designed to get you to think about how connected you are with your body, and whether you've got some work to do! The more connected we are to our body and how it feels, the better equipped we are to give it exactly what it wants. Health and wellness are about giving our body what it needs in order to feel better, and to do that, we have to be in touch with exactly what it needs. Sometimes, we are so used to treating it like a *machine* instead of the *vessel* that it is that we forget that it needs to be taken care of *gently*. It's the only "thing" we have for the rest of our lives, so we need to take good care of it.

*Think of a time when your body signaled something important to your mind (e.g., fatigue, pain, tension). How did you respond? What does this experience teach you about the connection between your body and mind?*

_______________________________________________

_______________________________________________

_______________________________________________

_______________________________________________

_______________________________________________

_______________________________________________

_______________________________________________

_______________________________________________

_______________________________________________

_______________________________________________

_______________________________________________

_______________________________________________

*Reflect on how stress manifests in your body. Where do you typically feel tension or discomfort when you're stressed? What does this tell you about how closely your physical and mental states are linked?*

*How does your physical health affect your ability to think clearly and make decisions? Recall a time when improving your physical health led to better mental clarity. What changes did you notice?*

*Identify a strong emotion you recently felt (e.g., anger, joy, sadness). How did your body react to this emotion? What does this reaction reveal about the interplay between your emotions and physical state?*

*Consider how often you "listen" to your body's signals. When was the last time you ignored your body's needs? What were the consequences, and how can you become more attuned to these signals?*

## Self-Care as an Act of Self-Respect

This section is about understanding that self-care is an act of self-respect. We tend to see self-care as something that involves a bubble bath or an extensive skin care routine, and yet, self-care doesn't have to be anything of the sort. It can be as simple as taking good care of yourself by doing your laundry if you have been avoiding doing it for some time. It can mean taking a whole weekend off work if you are self-employed and haven't had the time to just *relax* for a few days. It can also mean listening to your body when you don't want to go to the gym because you have had an exhausting day.

Self-care is self-respect because it means you are honoring how you feel and giving your body and mind the treatment they need to thrive and deserve! Take a look at the following questions and prompts and ask yourself whether you could make some changes to your self-care routine.

*How do you prioritize self-care in your daily life? Reflect on a time when you neglected self-care. What impact did it have on your well-being, and how can you ensure self-care becomes a non-negotiable part of your routine?*

*Think about your eating habits and how they reflect your level of self-respect. Are you feeding your body in a way that honors its needs? What changes can you make to better nourish yourself?*

*How do the boundaries you set (or fail to set) affect your self-care? Reflect on a situation where not setting boundaries drained you. What can you learn about respecting yourself through the boundaries you create?*

*What daily rituals do you have that show respect for your body and mind? Consider introducing a new ritual that would enhance your sense of self-respect. What might that be?*

*Self-care isn't just about physical acts; it's also about mental and emotional well-being. What are some ways you can care for your emotional and mental health daily? How do these practices show respect for yourself?*

## Healing Through Movement

You have already made tremendous progress towards building a strong connection between your mind and your body. You have also reflected on how you practice self-care and whether you could make some changes to your habits to treat yourself and your body better. Now, it's time to consider how you can use movement to heal.

Movement is an excellent way to change our mindset from one where we feel poorly to one where we feel inspired and full of energy, simply because it releases dopamine and makes us feel *good*. It likewise makes us feel accomplished, which is what we need at times to feel better about ourselves. However, movement can *also* be something that makes us feel poorly about ourselves if we overdo it, train while injured, or use exercise to punish ourselves—for eating, not being active enough, or because we dislike how we look. Movement should be *positive*. It should be associated with activities that make us feel *good*. It is something our bodies need to thrive and work at their best!

*Reflect on a time when physical movement helped you overcome an emotional or mental hurdle. What type of movement was it, and how did it help you heal or grow?*

*What forms of movement bring you the most joy? How does this joy translate into a sense of overall well-being? How can you incorporate more of this joyful movement into your life?*

*Think about a time when you used physical movement to release pent-up emotions. How did your body feel before and after? What does this experience teach you about the role of movement in emotional healing?*

*How does physical activity help you feel more connected to your body? Reflect on a recent experience where movement deepened your connection with yourself. What insights did you gain?*

*Consider the idea of movement as a form of spiritual practice. How can you incorporate mindfulness or a sense of sacredness into your physical activities? How might this shift change your experience of movement?*

# Part Two: Emotional Freedom

YOU MIGHT WONDER WHAT *emotional* and *mental* freedom—the latter being next on our list—have to do with wellness. Yet, many of us constantly feel poorly throughout life, at times more than others. Likewise, many of us feel like we are dependent on our emotions to lead us through life. If we feel good, things are going well. If we *don't* feel good, however, then things don't seem to be doing so well. Work gets harder. Being motivated to do the things we typically like doing gets more difficult. We don't know how to make ourselves feel better, because our usual habits are hard to get back on track with because these emotions are *so strong*. We might also blame ourselves for being unproductive, not being like that girl on social media who gets it all done, and we end up in a cycle where we feel like we're out of it—out of *control*. Things feel dull, and we don't know how to get out of this rut.

Well, a lot of these feelings can be there because we are stuck in past moments and on past emotions. The point of this workbook is to help you identify this and work on skills to get yourself *out of them*. Once this is achieved, you can apply this new positive feeling to other aspects of your life, and it all works like dominoes—one thing gets better, and then the next, and then the next... Getting yourself in a mindset and routine of health and wellness is *just as much* about your healthy habits relating to your *body* as it is about how you treat your *mind*.

## Releasing the Past

We all have past baggage. That's not a serious problem until it becomes something that completely stops us from moving forward. Do you feel like the way you were treated when you were younger may have had an impact on who you are today? Perhaps some of the beliefs that were transferred onto you by your parents, friends, or classmates as a child affected the way you view yourself? These early years are extremely important in building our sense of self and how we view ourselves today. So, we can't let ourselves continue to be held back by these feelings and views. Instead, we have to face them, acknowledge that they exist, and be willing to grow from them.

*What past experiences or memories still evoke strong emotions in you? How do these emotions affect your present life? What steps can you take to begin releasing the hold these past experiences have on you?*

*Think about someone or something you have yet to forgive. How does holding onto this resentment impact your emotional freedom? What would it look like to forgive and release this burden, even if only for your own peace?*

*Identify a story you've been telling yourself about your past. How does this story shape your current self-perception? What would change if you let go of this narrative and allowed yourself to create a new one?*

*Reflect on a painful experience from your past. How can you reframe this experience as an opportunity for growth or learning? What positive outcomes have come from moving through this pain?*

*Consider creating a ritual to symbolize letting go of something from your past. What could this ritual look like, and how might it help you emotionally move forward?*

27

## Emotional Vulnerability

Look, *no one* likes to feel vulnerable, unless they are surrounded by people, they feel they can trust. Vulnerability makes us scared of being hurt, which is why so many of us build up these tall, strong walls designed to keep people, events, or feelings out.

Yet, we are human beings, which means that by default, *we have emotions.* We have to be vulnerable enough to open up to people in order to form strong relationships with them. We have to be open to vulnerability to accept that there are things we care about deeply. So, consider the next few prompts, and ask yourself whether this aspect of your emotions might have been hindering your journey...

*Let's redefine vulnerability. How do you currently view vulnerability? Do you see it as a weakness or a strength? Reflect on a time when being vulnerable led to a positive outcome in your life. How did this experience change your perspective?*

*Think about a close relationship where you struggle to be fully vulnerable. What fears or concerns hold you back? How might embracing vulnerability in this relationship deepen your connection?*

*Reflect on an aspect of yourself that you usually hide from others. What would it take for you to reveal this part of yourself?*

*How might being more open and authentic lead to greater emotional freedom?*

*Consider a situation where you avoided speaking your truth because it made you feel too vulnerable. How did this choice affect you emotionally? What would have been different if you had embraced vulnerability and expressed yourself openly?*

*Think about a time when someone else's vulnerability inspired or comforted you. How can this experience encourage you to share your own struggles or fears? What might you gain from being more open?* 34

_____________________________________________________

_____________________________________________________

_____________________________________________________

_____________________________________________________

_____________________________________________________

_____________________________________________________

_____________________________________________________

_____________________________________________________

_____________________________________________________

_____________________________________________________

_____________________________________________________

_____________________________________________________

## Self-Compassion vs. Self-Criticism

The final aspect we are considering in this part is the idea of being more compassionate towards ourselves instead of being critical. We live in a world where comparison is all around us. We see people exceeding and doing amazing things, and sometimes, we feel like this is a sign that *we* aren't doing enough.

And yet, we all have our own lives. We all have things that we do that others wish they did, too. The grass is always greener on the other side. What if, instead of being critical of what you aren't doing, or that you aren't doing enough, you were *compassionate* and *understanding* of yourself? What if you focused on the *great things* you do and the amazing qualities you have instead of focusing on the things you don't have? What if you focused on the great things you want to achieve and the accomplishments you have had so far as opposed to the things you haven't done yet and regret not doing?

It's all a matter of perspective. To this end, the following prompts have been created to help you identify how you can show yourself more *compassion*, as opposed to being too *critical* of yourself.

*How do you speak to yourself when you make a mistake or fall short of your expectations? Is your inner dialogue more compassionate or critical? Reflect on how changing this dialogue could impact your emotional well-being.*

*Identify a recent situation where you were hard on yourself. How might you have approached it differently with self-compassion? What specific things could you say or do to be kinder to yourself in similar situations?*

_______________________________________________

_______________________________________________

_______________________________________________

_______________________________________________

_______________________________________________

_______________________________________________

_______________________________________________

_______________________________________________

_______________________________________________

_______________________________________________

_______________________________________________

_______________________________________________

*How do you balance striving for self-improvement with accepting yourself as you are? Reflect on an area of your life where you feel stuck between self-criticism and self-compassion. What would it look like to find harmony between these two approaches?*

*Consider the role self-criticism plays in your life. While it can be harmful, are there ways it has helped you grow or learn? How can you acknowledge these benefits while still cultivating more self-compassion?*

___________________________________________

___________________________________________

___________________________________________

___________________________________________

___________________________________________

___________________________________________

___________________________________________

___________________________________________

___________________________________________

___________________________________________

___________________________________________

___________________________________________

*What would change if you allowed yourself to be imperfect and embraced self-compassion instead?*

# Part Three: Mental Freedom

IT'S UNFORTUNATE, BUT MANY of us are often trapped in our own thoughts and in the beliefs that we have accumulated over the years. These beliefs are found in many aspects of our lives: how we think we come across to other people, how talented we believe we are, whether we believe that we can achieve our dreams, how we feel about our bodies, and many, many more! These internal beliefs can therefore do one of two things: they can support us in our journey towards the kind of life that we are building for ourselves, or they can hold us back from doing all the amazing things we dream of!

This part is all about addressing these limiting beliefs, particularly in the first section. Second, we will look at how you can incorporate more mindfulness so you become aware of how you feel, when these beliefs are creeping up, and what you can do about them. Third, we will start detaching ourselves from external validation. We will stop relying on *others' approval* to feel good about ourselves. Instead, we will focus on what *we* can do in order to feel good and positive about ourselves. We will focus on the parts of ourselves that make us feel proud of who we are and what we have accomplished. We will build inner confidence and redefine what it means to be successful on our *own terms*.

## Breaking Free from Limiting Beliefs

We're starting with these limiting beliefs—the beliefs that tell you that you cannot do something or aren't good enough. They are the beliefs that make you feel like you won't achieve the dreams you have. They are the beliefs to keep in check and to challenge when they come up, because they are not *true*; they are based on preconceptions you have of yourself, or self-esteem struggles that *can* be addressed.

*Reflect on a belief you hold about yourself that you suspect might be limiting your potential. How has this belief influenced your decisions and actions? What evidence can you find that challenges the validity of this belief?*

*Consider how fear of change might be connected to a limiting belief. What changes have you avoided because of this belief? How can you confront this fear and begin to embrace change as a path to growth?*

*Imagine what your life would look like if you didn't hold onto any limiting beliefs. What would you pursue? How would you behave differently? Reflect on one small step you can take today to move toward this vision.*

*Think about a story you've been telling yourself that reinforces a limiting belief. How can you rewrite this story to reflect your true potential and capabilities?*

*What new narrative will you start telling yourself today?*

*Reflect on a time when a limiting belief led you to perceive an obstacle as insurmountable. How can you reframe that obstacle as an opportunity for growth or learning?*

*What can you do to start seeing challenges as opportunities rather than barriers?*

## Mindfulness — Your Path to Being Mentally Liberated

Mindfulness is more than just something related to the "very mindful, very demure" TikTok trend of 2024. It is something we should use in our daily life! It is the act of being aware of the way we feel, think, and *what stands behind* these thoughts and feelings. Being mindful helps you become more in touch with who you really *are* and what you really *want*, which helps you get out of that rut you have been in and helps you feel empowered to do all the amazing things you want to do in your life! Being mindful helps you liberate yourself from the beliefs you have or the thoughts that tell you not to do something. It helps you feel excited for the future again. It's part of a wellness and health routine, and something that can bring you more clarity on the things you want to do so badly in your life. It helps you stop *existing* and motivates you to start really *living*.

*How often do you find yourself dwelling on the past or worrying about the future? Reflect on how practicing mindfulness—being fully present in the moment—could help you gain mental freedom.*

*What simple mindfulness practice can you begin integrating into your daily life?*

*Consider how often you judge your own thoughts or emotions. How might observing them without judgment lead to greater mental freedom? Try practicing non-judgmental observation for a day and reflect on how it affects your mental state.*

*Reflect on the power of your breath to influence your mental state. How can focusing on your breath during moments of stress or anxiety help you achieve mental clarity and freedom? Practice mindful breathing and note its impact on your thoughts and emotions.*

*Think about how you can bring mindfulness into everyday tasks like eating, walking, or even washing dishes. How does paying full attention to these activities change your experience of them? How might this practice contribute to your overall sense of mental freedom?*

*Reflect on the mental clutter you carry—thoughts, worries, or distractions that take up space in your mind. How can mindfulness help you clear this clutter and focus on what truly matters?*

*What steps can you take to declutter your mind today?*

# Detach Yourself from External Validation

The final area of your life that we will be tackling is that of *external validation*. We all care about what others think about us, or what they say about us behind our backs. It's only normal. We *want* to be accepted and loved as we are, and we *want* people to see us as the best versions of ourselves.

However, *depending* on external validation can also mean that we end up doing things we don't really want to do, just because we *think* that's what we're meant to do. We *think* we need people to approve of what we're doing; otherwise, it means we're not doing the right thing. We *think* we have to be validated by others, even if in reality, we have all the validation we need inside ourselves. To be *truly* happy, healthy, and well, you have to trust that the decisions you are making are *yours*. You have to feel empowered to choose to do what works best for you, regardless of what you think others want you to do. You have to be strong, and you have to stand by your convictions. That's how you start building true confidence.

*Reflect on a recent decision you made. How much of it was influenced by a desire for external approval? How might your choice have been different if you were guided solely by your own values and desires? What does this tell you about your relationship with external validation?*

*Think about an area of your life where you rely heavily on external validation. How can you start building confidence from within, independent of others' opinions? What practices or affirmations can help you reinforce this inner confidence?*

*Consider how much your definition of success is shaped by societal standards or the expectations of others. What would success look like if it were defined purely by your own values and passions? How can you start living according to this personal definition?*

*Reflect on the idea that your worth is not determined by external achievements or others' opinions. How can you cultivate a sense of inherent self-worth? What daily practices can help you internalize the belief that you are enough, just as you are?*

*Think about a situation where you felt pressured to conform to others' expectations rather than being true to yourself. How did this affect your sense of freedom?*

# The Last Step: Your Five-Year Plan

WELL, YOU'VE DONE IT. You have completed this workbook. You have asked yourself *all* the difficult questions and have grown tremendously. You have developed a new version of yourself, one that is confident and ready to start implementing changes to your health, wellness, and wellbeing. Now, it's time to put all these new skills into action, and to plan out what you will do in the next five years to arrive there.

This is an exercise for you to consider *exactly what you want to be doing*. So, you need to be honest with yourself, and you have to visualize yourself being exactly where you want to be.

First, start by imagining where you are five years from now. Think of all the details—whether you live on the beach, in the mountains, in a city. You choose. Then, think of what your daily life looks like. Are you working for yourself? Working at a job you love? Are you retired because you saved a lot of money and gave yourself that freedom?

Next, think of your morning routine. How do you start your day? Do you wake up next to someone? Are you drinking your favorite coffee?

Next, think of your day in general. What are you doing? How do you *feel* while doing it? Are you proud of yourself? Do you feel accomplished? Why is that?

Importantly, how do you take care of yourself? What's your exercise routine like? How do you eat? What do you look like? How does your body feel? What does it allow you to do? Do you take a minute to be mindful and grateful for all the things it allows you to do, like walk down the street, grab a coffee, and go back home? Do you thank it for allowing you to climb mountains, or stand up at important meetings? Do you show your gratitude by treating it with love and respect?

Then, at the end of the night, what do you do? How do you close the evening? Do you squeeze in a PM workout? What do you cook for dinner? How do you decompress from the day?

Once you have this picture in your mind and it is crystal-clear, start planning. How will you get there? How will you break down these goals into smaller, more achievable ones? What will you *do* to get there? What can you do today to get one step closer? What about tomorrow? What about this month? Break down these goals into yearly chunks. Then, again, do this for six months. And three months. And monthly, and weekly. Then, get to work.

You've got this.